S0-ABQ-594

RANDY'S CORNER

DAY BY DAY WITH...

TAYLOR SWIFT

BY
KAYLEEN REUSSER

Mitchell Lane
PUBLISHERS

P.O. Box 196
Hockessin, Delaware 19707
Visit us on the web: www.mitchelllane.com
Comments? email us:
mitchelllane@mitchelllane.com

Mitchell Lane
PUBLISHERS

Printing   3   4   5   6   7   8   9

RANDY'S CORNER

DAY BY DAY WITH . . .

Beyoncé	Miley Cyrus
Dwayne "The Rock" Johnson	Selena Gomez
Eli Manning	Shaun White
Justin Bieber	Taylor Swift
LeBron James	Willow Smith

Library of Congress Cataloging-in-Publication Data
Reusser, Kayleen.
  Day by day with Taylor Swift / by Kayleen Reusser.
     p. cm. — (Randy's corner)
  Includes bibliographical references and index.
  ISBN 978-1-58415-857-8 (library bound)
 1. Swift, Taylor, 1989—Juvenile literature. 2. Women country musicians—
United States—Biography—Juvenile literature. 3. Singers—United States—
Biography—Juvenile literature. I. Title.
  ML3930.S989R57 2010
  782.421642092—dc22
  [B]
                                                              2010006534

ABOUT THE AUTHOR: Kayleen Reusser has written several books for Mitchell Lane, including biographies *Taylor Swift*, *Selena Gomez*, and *Leona Lewis* for older readers. She works in a public middle school library and loves speaking to students about writing. Reusser lives with her family in the Midwest. Learn more about her at http://www.KayleenR.com.

PUBLISHER'S NOTE: The following story has been thoroughly researched, and to the best of our knowledge represents a true story. While every possible effort has been made to ensure accuracy, the publisher will not assume liability for damages caused by inaccuracies in the data and makes no warranty on the accuracy of the information contained herein. This story has not been authorized or endorsed by Taylor Swift.

PLB / PLB2 / PLB2

DAY BY DAY WITH

TAYLOR SWIFT

Taylor Swift grew up in Pennsylvania. As a young girl, she dreamed of being a country music singer.

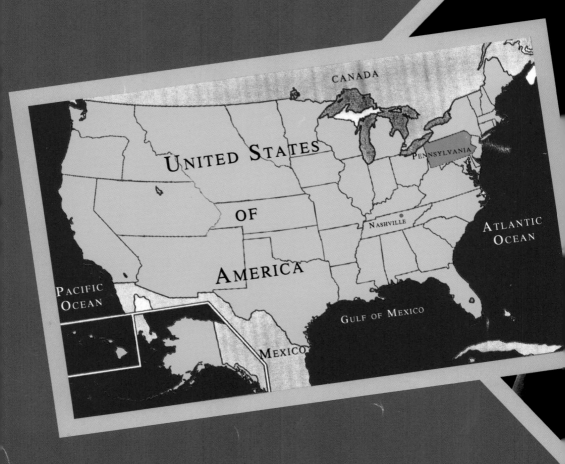

CANADA

UNITED STATES

OF

AMERICA

PENNSYLVANIA

NASHVILLE

PACIFIC
OCEAN

ATLANTIC
OCEAN

GULF OF MEXICO

MEXICO

After Taylor learned to play guitar, she began writing songs.

A few years later, her family moved to Nashville, Tennessee, where she found a job writing tunes for a record company.

People enjoyed Taylor's songs. She wrote about things she knew, like friends, boys, and school.

When Scott Borchetta heard Taylor sing, he offered her a recording contract. Taylor knew she was on her way to being a country music star!

TAYLOR WATCHES HER COMMERCIAL

Taylor wrote all of the songs on her first album. She sang them on TV and at large stadiums around the country.

BRETT RATNER, DIRECTOR

She became so popular that she was asked to work on exciting projects, like the Band Hero commercial she made with Brett Ratner.

As Taylor's music began to be played on the radio, she performed for bigger and bigger crowds. At first, she was afraid to sing for thousands of people. But the more Taylor sang, the more she loved it!

In 2008, Taylor was asked to sing the national anthem at a World Series baseball game. By that time, she had sung hundreds of songs for people.

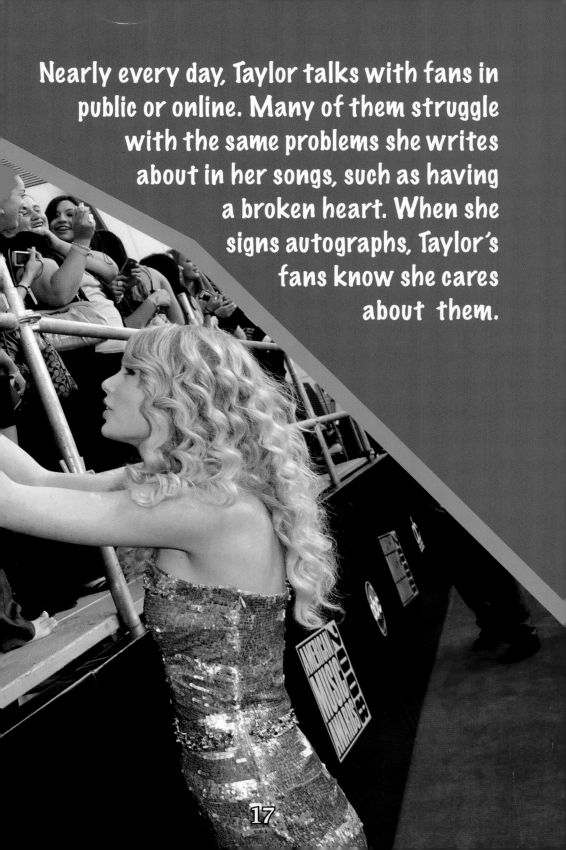

Nearly every day, Taylor talks with fans in public or online. Many of them struggle with the same problems she writes about in her songs, such as having a broken heart. When she signs autographs, Taylor's fans know she cares about them.

TAYLOR

JOE

Taylor uses her time on the road to meet friends like Joe Jonas and Miley Cyrus.

Traveling from city to city on tour can be lonely for Taylor. Her mother, Andrea, goes with her. Taylor's dad, Scott, and brother, Austin, usually stay at home.

TAYLOR & MILEY

TAYLOR & MOM

Another friend of Taylor's is Selena Gomez, star of the TV show *The Wizards of Waverly Place*. Selena is a singer and actress. Taylor and Selena know that being popular is exciting, but their families and friends will support and love them, no matter what happens.

Sometimes people are surprised by how tall Taylor is. At 5 feet, 11 inches, she is as tall as many men. Taylor doesn't mind being tall—singers can be any height!

During concerts, Taylor likes to wear dresses and boots. When she shops, she looks for clothes that are pretty and that she feels comfortable wearing.

Taylor helps others in many ways. She donated a pink truck to a camp for sick kids. She also gave $100,000 to the Red Cross to help families who lost their homes in tornadoes and floods.

VICTORY JUNCTION GANG.

Founded for kids in honor of Adam Petty

Taylor donates clothes to a group that provides teen girls with prom dresses. (A prom is a formal dance event held at most high schools).

DONATING TO THE RED CROSS

JAY LENO

Taylor talks to many people who work at radio and television stations. They ask her about being a country music star. She hopes her answers will help listeners understand her goal. She wants to be the best country music singer in the nation.

Taylor has become one of the busiest singers in the United States. People write about her in books, newspapers, and magazines. There is always something new to learn about this talented singer from Pennsylvania.

FURTHER READING

Works Consulted

Finan, Eileen. "Country Girl Talk." *People*, September 15, 2008. http://www.people.com/people/archive/article/0,,20230670,00.html.

Forr, Amanda. "Fabulously Fearless." *Girls' Life*, December/January 2009, pp. 50–54. http://findarticles.com/p/articles/mi_m0IBX/is_3_15/ai_n31162799/

Grigoriadis, Vanessa. "The Very Pink, Very Perfect Life of Taylor Swift." *Rolling Stone*, February 19, 2009, pp. 44–51. http://www.rollingstone.com/news/coverstory/26213623

Scarola, Danielle. "Taylor's Love Lessons." *Girls' Life*, February/March 2010, pp. 50–53.

"Six Random Things Taylor Swift Loves." *InStyle*, January 2010. http://www.instyle.com/instyle/package/grammys/photos/0,,20337197_20326242_20710276,00.html

Willman, Chris. "American Girl." *Entertainment Weekly*, February 8, 2008.

On the Internet

CMT (Country Music Television) Get Country
http://www.cmt.com/artists/az/swift__taylor/artist.jhtml

Taylor Swift Official Facebook Page
http://www.facebook.com/TaylorSwift?v=app_19935916616

Taylor Swift Official MySpace
http://www.myspace.com/taylorswift

Taylor Swift Official Website
www.taylorswift.com

INDEX

PHOTO CREDITS: Cover design—Joe Rasemas; Cover—AP Photo/Mark J. Terrill; p. 3—Theo Wargo/WireImage/Getty Images; pp. 4, 19 (top)—Rick Diamond/Getty Images; p. 6—AP Photo/Evan Agostini; p. 8—Ethan Miller/Getty Images; pp. 10, 16—Kevin Winter/Getty Images; p. 12—Jason Squires/WireImage/Getty Images; p. 14—John Mabangalo-Pool/Getty Images; p. 18—Jeff Kravitz/FilmMagic/Getty Images; p. 19 (bottom)—Frazer Harrison/ACMA/Getty Images; p. 20—Todd Williamson/WireImage/Getty Images; pp. 22, 30—AP Photo/Peter Kramer; p. 24—Jean Baptiste Lacroix/WireImage/Getty Images; p. 26—Barbara Marvis; p. 28—NBCU Photo Bank/AP Photo/Paul Drinkwater. Every effort has been made to locate all copyright holders of materials used in this book. Any errors or omissions will be corrected in future editions of the book.